CLB 1790
First published in Great Britain by Colour Library Books Ltd.,
    Guildford, Surrey, England.
© 1986 Text: Colour Library Books Ltd.
© 1986 Illustrations: Rex Features, David Levenson/Colorific,
    Colour Library Books, Photo Source and Camera Press.
Printed and bound in Barcelona. Spain by Cronion, S.A.
ISBN 0 86283 488 0
Dep. Leg. B-27.613-86

THE BOOK OF THE
ROYAL WEDDING

*The armorial bearings of Prince Andrew, showing the Royal Arms
surrounded by the Chain of the Royal Victorian Order, which the Queen
personally conferred upon him.*

COLOUR LIBRARY BOOKS
86 Epsom Road, Guildford, Surrey GU1 2BX
Telephone (0483) 579191

The photographs in this book will remind you of a day of royal splendour, and bring back some of the beauty of colour and sound which made this wedding, in the incomparable setting of Westminster Abbey, an occasion to lift the heart.

Although millions were watching on television, those of us who took part were chiefly concerned to make the marriage service a memorable and even intimate event in the lives of the two people who were at the centre of it.

As it happened, I was installed as Dean of Westminster between two weddings which, in different ways, were of great significance to me. The previous week, in my church in Cambridge, I officiated at the wedding of my own daughter – also Sarah – and shared the joy of two people, deeply in love, making a lifelong commitment to each other.

The setting of that wedding, and that of the Royal Wedding a fortnight after my installation, could not have been more different. But at the heart of each event were the same words, the same emotions, and the same joy of two separate people beginning the mysterious process of becoming what the Bible calls 'one flesh'.

To believe in marriage is to believe that a man and a woman can commit themselves in a lifelong relationship of unconditional love. They make promises which are binding, and each accepts responsibility for the other, in good days and bad – a commitment strong enough to survive the occasional rows and misunderstandings which are part of the long process of growing together.

The relationship can be enormously difficult, but where it succeeds it is uniquely rewarding. It calls for openness, for absolute trust and loyalty, and not least for a mutual cherishing and encouragement of each other. It calls for a quality of love which, in St Paul's words, 'is always patient... which does not take offence, is not resentful... and is always ready to excuse, to trust, to hope and to endure'.

For each to say to the other, within the trusting security of marriage, *I give myself to you unconditionally* does not diminish them as individuals, but enhances them, for in marriage we complement each other and, in a mysterious way, need each other to become our true selves.

Every wedding witnesses to this vision of the love between two people creating that which is new and life-giving; a setting in which children can grow and flourish. It gives us something to celebrate. At a Royal Wedding we celebrate the same truth, but on an infinitely larger canvas.

Michael Mayne
Dean of Westminster

Introduction

It is interesting to reflect that, of the twelve countries comprising the European Economic Community, six are happily ruled by Kings, Queens or, in one case, by a reigning Grand Duke. Their political structures are in fact constitutional monarchies, where the monarch is head of state but with little direct political power. We in Britain have evolved this excellent form of government since the Revolution of 1688, and now our Queen plays a considerable part in ruling her United Kingdom (and, indeed, the Commonwealth) where her rights have been so well described by Bagehot as 'to be consulted, to encourage and to warn'.

It cannot go unnoticed that the republican countries of Europe greatly envy us our continuing royal heritage. Indeed, they so often proudly refer to their own history by highlighting the deeds and reigns of *their* powerful kings, such as Louis XIV of France. Perhaps the greatest hero in French history was Napoleon I, whom Frenchmen idolise as their Emperor – even though he was born in Corsica and, starting as a young artillery officer, grew to power through various *coups d'état*. How comparatively tawdry and dull are the trappings that surround a president of a republic against the splendour and royal traditions of a monarchy, and how lucky we are to have a Royal Family which remains united and whose every family event, such as this memorable wedding of Prince Andrew and Miss Sarah Ferguson, becomes an occasion of national rejoicing and happiness.

Many people think that the Earl Marshal is responsible for the ceremonial of royal marriages, but this is not the case: he has not organised royal weddings since the days of Queen Anne. Subsequent weddings have been the responsibility of the Lord Chamberlain because Georgian and Victorian weddings of the Royal Family usually took place inside the royal palaces themselves. This reflects the division of responsibility of the medieval Officers of the Court. The Earl Marshal's was originally a military role, and he is therefore still responsible for some of the external ceremonial activities of the monarch – State occasions such as the Investiture of the Prince of Wales at Caernarfon Castle, the Opening of Parliament, the funeral of Sir Winston Churchill and, of course the greatest of all State occasions, the Coronation of the Sovereign. Broadly speaking, the Lord Chamberlain looks after the other activities of the Sovereign, the royal palaces and the organisation of events within their walls. By implication, this essentially private royal wedding is one of those events.

Finally, we Yorkshiremen rejoice in all the popular clamour for the creation of Prince Andrew as Duke of York – a title taken from the second city of England, ranking immediately after London as one of the few cities which have a Lord Mayor. And York's coat of arms, so simple and so historic with its red cross of St George and the lions of the Plantagenet kings, bears ample witness to our royal heritage.

I am delighted to have had this opportunity to set down these few thoughts to introduce this colourful and informative book to you. I am sure that, as you turn its pages, you will enjoy its lively text and brilliant illustrations, and will come to value it for many years as a superb, lasting memento of a glorious day in the life of our Royal Family.

Miles, Duke of Norfolk
Earl Marshal of England

A brief glimpse at the Royal Family's wedding albums: (right and top) Princess Elizabeth and the Duke of Edinburgh in 1947; (above) Princess Anne and Capt Mark Phillips in November 1973, where almost 40 relatives were pictured (opposite, top). (Left) Prince Charles' wedding in 1981.

Pages and bridesmaids always steal the show: (above) Prince Edward and Lady Sarah Armstrong-Jones at Princess Anne's wedding; (top left) Princess Margaret with her bridesmaids in 1960; (left centre) Princess Diana's little helpers leaving St Paul's after her marriage to Prince Charles (opposite) — an occasion which showed the Prince at his most affectionate (left and top).

Previous pages: Sarah, the working girl, and enjoying the company of Princess Diana, at polo. (Left) the Ferguson family home, Dummer Down Farm, in Hampshire. (Right) Sloane turned Princess-to-be: Sarah's official engagement portrait contrasts with the informality of her bachelor-girl days (pictures below) and the casual light-heartedness of her engagement (overleaf). (Following pages) Sarah visits Andrew on board HMS Brazen (left) just before their engagement and (right) accompanies him at a clay-pigeon shoot in July.

Horse laughs: Andrew and Sarah's pleasant Spring afternoon at the Windsor Horse Show, just a short drive away from Windsor Castle. Royalty rarely relaxes more fully than when surrounded by horses, and Sarah's reactions to the day's thrills and spills made it evident that she is very much at home sharing the Royal Family's favourite fascination.

Both Sarah and Andrew are connoisseurs of the horse world, and the public had its first opportunity to see them in a relaxed setting at the Horse Show. It was hardly the most glamorous of occasions, with the royal couple and the Queen well wrapped up in woollies and wellies against a cold, damp and unseasonal May afternoon.

A windblown Sarah (above) with the Queen and Prince Andrew at the Windsor Horse Show. (Opposite page, insets) arriving for the final day's events, and watching from the royal box as the three day event comes to its close.

(Previous pages) a kiss from Andrew on her engagement day; a glimpse of the royal ruby-and-diamond engagement ring; and a huge bow ribbon for one of Sarah's first official outings with Andrew. (These pages) High fashion at Ascot: Sarah with Princess Margaret (top), Princess Anne (above) and (opposite page) the Queen Mother and Princess Michael.

Sarah almost lost in a sea of faces (below) as she follows the Queen in the Royal Enclosure at Ascot, and (left and right) wearing a Texan-sized hat. (Bottom) Andrew with his parents and elder brother on their way to the Royal Enclosure. (Overleaf) Sarah arrives with Andrew to watch a charity theatre production in Weymouth.

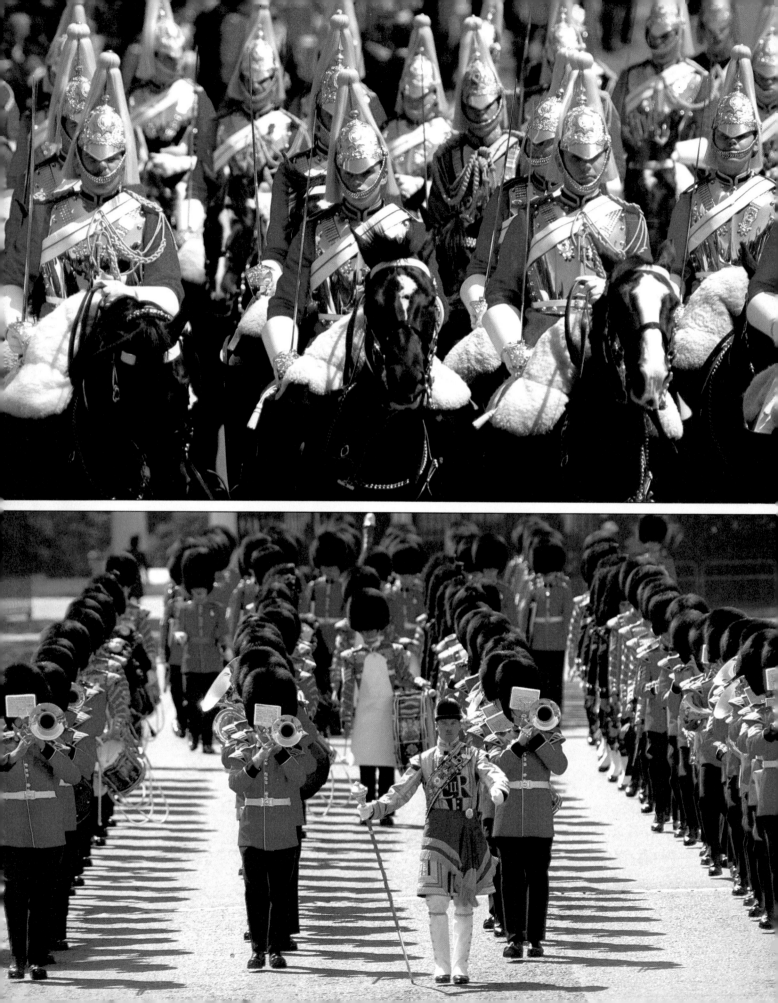

Nearly one of the family: Sarah appears (top) for the second time on the Palace balcony, after the Queen's birthday parade (left and overleaf) in June, along with seasoned royals like the Queen Mother (right), Princess Diana and Princess Michael of Kent (above).

(Right) Another formal engagement portrait, by Terence Donovan. The London Season saw Sarah enjoying a variety of public outings. (Top) at Wimbledon in June; (above and left) at the wedding of her former flatmate in July; (overleaf, left) at the Jackie Stewart Celebrity Clay-Pigeon Shoot in July; (overleaf, right) sumptuously dressed at an evening engagement with Andrew; and (following pages) with her father and Andrew at Smith's Lawn, Windsor during Ascot Week.

K.Y.C. RESCUE

(Previous page) All smiles for Sarah and Andrew during a visit to Northern Ireland in June. (These pages). Andrew looks on proudly as Sarah presents the Queen's Cup to Prince Charles' victorious polo team that month. (Overleaf) Sarah sporting some of her more complicated millinery at a friend's summer wedding in London.

THE ROYAL W

23rd J

ANDREW
DUKE OF
YORK

EDDING DAY
ly 1986

SARAH
DUCHESS OF YORK

London was a patriot's delight on the wedding day, with impromptu demonstrations of loyalty all along the route before the groom and his brother emerged into public view.

If you had a flag to wave, a message to send, Union Jack clothes to wear, a song to sing and plenty of red, white and blue to spray on your face, then their wedding day was also your day. Though July 23rd was not an official holiday, both young and old made it their excuse for a rare spot of innocent fun.

A momentary change in the weather as the royal carriages arrive at Sanctuary Green. Though it stayed favourable, the occasional black cloud kept crowds alert for the odd shower. Meanwhile an airship bearing a "Good Luck" message hovered above Parliament (left).

A mile of smiles from Prince Andrew and Prince Edward (right) as they journeyed towards Westminster Abbey via Parliament Square (left). No corner of the royal route was devoid of crowds and Trafalgar Square (top) was an especially popular vantage point.

Crowds caught just a glimpse of Sarah's top-secret wedding dress as she rode in the Glass Coach with her father. (Following pages) a smiling Queen and Prince Philip arrive for the service.

Royalty and other guests, including Nancy Reagan arrived at the Abbey with studied punctuality. Following pages: Major Ronald Ferguson and Sarah's dressmaker, Lindka Cierach, made final adjustments to her train.

When her carriage stopped at the Abbey (above) Sarah was 20 minutes away from becoming Duchess of York. Her 17$\frac{1}{2}$-foot-long train gave occasional problems but her progress up the aisle to the Sacrarium (following page) was measured and confident. So was her return, to face in-laws clearly delighted to count her as one of them.

"I'll tell you one thing," Sarah said just before her wedding; "there'll be nothing else like it." She was talking of her wedding dress and she was proved right on the day. Pearl and sequin embroidery and interwoven initials, crests and designs were its hallmarks. No wonder she was smiling (right)!

Royalty and little helpers in waiting before and during the service. (Above right) Ronald Ferguson with bride and groom at the sanctuary rail. (Opposite) the triumphant bridal walk down the aisle.

Like all royal brides before her, Sarah's last duty before she walked from the Sacrarium was to curtsey to the Queen, a manoeuvre achieved (top left) with supreme aplomb and a broad smile! Prince William led the pages and bridesmaids out after her (above), while the camera caught a rare Fergie grimace as she tried to lift her billowing dress and train back into the carriage (right).

The sun shone, briefly, as Sarah and Andrew emerged from beneath the blue awning with its distinctive white-stripe trimming, past a guard of honour formed by forty seamen who had once served on the same ships as the groom. For the first time the public had a full and lingering view of Sarah's magnificent dress.

(Right) Andrew and Sarah walk past their sailor guard to await
their carriage (left). Andrew helps (above left) with her long
train before (top) she climbs into the coach.

Sarah and Andrew are first out of the Abbey (above right) and quickly away while other members of the Royal Family await their carriages – among them, the Queen, Queen Mother, Prince and Princess of Wales and Princess Anne (above left), and Prince and Princess Michael of Kent with their children, Freddie and Ella (top).

It was a sunny and light-hearted drive back to Buckingham Palace and both Sarah and Andrew enjoyed the heady atmosphere to the full. At the end of their first journey together as man and wife, Sarah's first act was to give each of her bridesmaids and pages a huge kiss — and they couldn't line up fast enough to be on the receiving end.

The happy couple homeward bound (above and left) in
pleasant, warm sunshine, followed by the Queen with Major
Ferguson (seen, top right, leaving the Abbey) and Prince Philip,
in cheerful and animated conversation (right) with Sarah's
mother. The crowd lost no time, of course, in taking over the
Mall when the carriages had passed.

Prince Edward (top) takes charge of bridesmaids and pages, while the Queen Mother (above) travels in more sedate company. (Opposite) Sarah and Andrew find time for a quick word amid all the cheering.

Wide hats (the Queen, Princess Margaret, Lady Sarah Armstrong-Jones, Princess Anne and Mrs Barrantes) set the fashion for the day as the royal carriage procession winds back to Buckingham Palace. And many senior members of the Royal Family, including the Queen, Queen Mother, Princess Margaret and Princess Alice, wore blue.

Triumphal processions follow the bride and groom (above left) back to the Palace. The elder bridesmaids and pages (left) are followed by Prince Philip with Mrs. Susan Barrantes (top & right) mother of the bride, and by the Queen Mother with Princess Margaret and her children.

Two hands raised as one (right) as Andrew and Sarah head for home, via Trafalgar Square and Admiralty Arch (left). Charles and Diana (above) seem more cautious, while the Queen hangs on to her hat (above right) in a stiffish breeze as she drove back with Sarah's father. Top: Princess Anne and her husband in carefree mood.

No.	When Married.	Name and Surname.	Age.	Condition.	Rank or Profession.	Residence at the time of Marriage.	Father's Name and Surname.	Rank or Profession of Father.
419	23rd July 1986	Andrew Albert Christian Edward Mountbatten-Windsor	26	Bachelor	Prince of the United Kingdom of Great Britain and Northern Ireland Duke of York	Buckingham Palace	His Royal Highness The Prince Philip.	Duke of Edinburgh KG OM
		Sarah Margaret Ferguson	26	Spinster	Publisher	Dummer Down House Dummer Basingstoke Hampshire	Ronald Ivor Ferguson	Farmer

1986. Marriage solemnized at *Westminster Abbey* in the *Close* of *St Peter: Westminster* in the County of *London*

Married in *Westminster Abbey* according to the Rites and Ceremonies of the *Established Church* by *Special Licence* by me,

This Marriage was solemnized between us,

Andrew
Sarah Ferguson.

Robert Cantuarens

in the presence of us:—

Elizabeth R
Philip
Anne
Mark Phillips
Peter Phillips

Elizabeth R
Edward
Richard Brigitte
Mora Rose Alice
Davina

Charles
Diana
Ronald Ferguson
Susan 'bode' Barrantes.
Margaret Michael
Sarah Armstrong-Jones
Kinley *Ella*
Alexandra

Michael Wayne dean
William & Edward
Harry.
James Ogilvy
Katharine Marina Ophelia
St Andrew
Helen Jones
Marie-Christine Alice
Seamus
Frederick
Angus Ogilvy And. Zara

Everybody in the family put their name on the register (top) though Princess Diana wrote in William's and Harry's for them. And all appeared on the balcony (above and left) from which the novices must have been amazed at the sight of hundreds of thousands surging down the Mall towards them (right).

New faces on the balcony (top) include Major Ferguson, Seamus Makim, Andrew Ferguson, Mrs Barrantes, Lady Rosanagh Innes-Ker, Laura Fellowes – and, of course, the bride. Gallant Prince Andrew gives his wife a helping hand (above) with her train as they go back inside, leaving the crowd to drift away (left).

The Royal Standard (top picture) flying high over Buckingham Palace as the crowds swarm round to see the bride and groom on the balcony. Prince Harry didn't attend the service but (right) was given a good view of the crowds below. For the rest there was a lot of waving and pointing as banners bearing witty messages were raised high.

Previous page: a balcony of royals.
These pages: Sarah and Andrew indulge in a
kiss and a moment's fun with the crowd.
Overleaf: eyes front, 47 times, for the official
photograph.

What a day for the bridesmaids and pages to remember – and what picture to remember it by (left). It ended with a carriage drive at spanking pace from the Palace to Chelsea Royal Hospital, marked in the fashionable royal way by the unofficial placard and L-plate (above) and in the time-honoured, though not exclusively royal way by handfuls of confetti being thrown into the landau (right).

Members of the Royal Family mingle with chefs, footmen, maids and valets to send the new Duke and Duchess of York off in grand style. The Queen, in particularly good humour, actually ran after the carriage as it moved off with its decorative bunting, drawn by four of her Windsor Greys.

Sarah's cascading dress contrasts with the splendours of the Throne Room and Andrew's sober uniform in this classic formal study (above). Much less formally (opposite), the newlyweds leave for honeymoon, teddy-bear in tow!

The final ceremony on a day of ceremonies was by royal standards pretty informal. Andrew and Sarah arrived (right) at the Royal Hospital, Chelsea, where the bride received a bouquet (above right). Then it was into the royal red helicopter for an 11–minute flight to London Airport and a well-deserved honeymoon.